Building **Grade 2**
SPELLING
Skills Daily Practice

Spelling Strategies

▶ Say a word correctly.

▶ Think about what the word looks like.

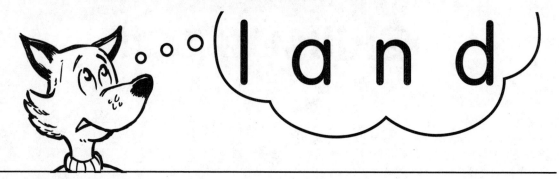

▶ Look for small words in spelling words.

▶ Use rhyming words to help spell a word.

land hand sand

How to Study Your List

1 Read and Spell

2 Copy and Spell

3 Cover and Spell

4 Uncover and Check

Good for me!

Spelling List

This Week's Focus:
- Spell short vowel words

STEP 1 Read and Spell

STEP 2 Copy and Spell

STEP 3 Cover and Spell

fold

1. on

2. not

3. but

4. at

5. had

6. in

7. did

8. get

9. red

10. hot

11. _____
   bonus word

12. _____
   bonus word

Fill in the boxes.

on   not   but   at   had

in   did   get   red   hot

1.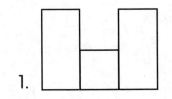

2.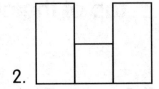

3.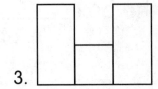

4.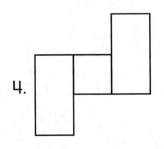

5.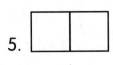

6.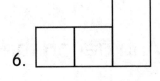

7.

8.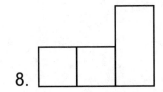

9.

10.

Find the Mistakes

Mark an **X** on the misspelled words.

1. The pan is ~~hat~~.

2. A dog is un the bed.

3. Can I git a cat?

4. His hat is read.

Word Meaning

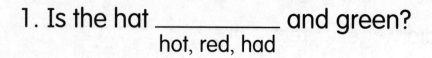

Write the missing word on the line.

1. Is the hat _____ and green?
   hot, red, had

2. Set the box _____ top of the desk.
   in, at, on

3. Can you _____ a cup for me?
   get, but, hot

4. _____ Ann get on the bus?
   Not, Did, Had

5. His pizza is _____.
   but, hot, not

6. Dad _____ to fix the car.
   in, at, had

My Spelling Dictation

Write the sentences.
Circle the spelling words.

1. _____

   _____

2. _____

   _____

Word Study

Read the words. Listen for the short vowel sounds.
Write each word in the correct box.

on	in	not	did	but
get	at	hot	red	had
cup	sit	men	pan	up

short **a**	short **e**	short **i**	short **o**	short **u**
_____	_____	_____	_____	_____
_____	_____	_____	_____	_____
_____	_____	_____	_____	_____
_____	_____	_____	_____	_____

Change one letter to make a spelling word.

1. dot

_____ hot _____

2. sad

_____

3. lid

_____

4. nut

_____

5. pet

_____

6. bed

_____

Spelling List

This Week's Focus:
- Spell short vowel words

STEP 1 Read and Spell

STEP 2 Copy and Spell

STEP 3 Cover and Spell

fold

1. as

2. has

3. fox

4. box

5. mix

6. egg

7. jam

8. pet

9. nap

10. big

11. _____
    bonus word

12. _____
    bonus word

Visual Memory

Fill in the boxes.

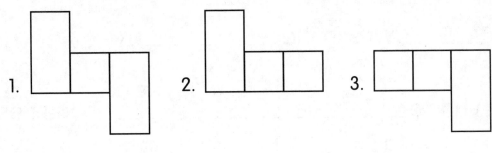

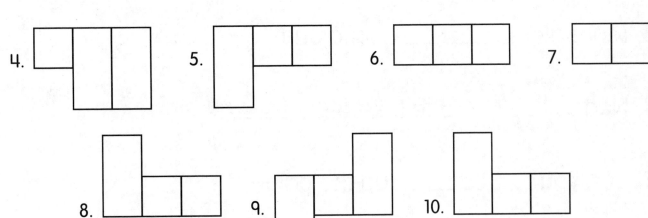

Spell Vowel Sounds

Fill in the missing vowel to make a spelling word. Write **a**, **e**, **i**, **o**, or **u**.

f_o_x   j__m   b__x

__gg   __s   h__s

m__x   n__p   p__t

Fill in the missing words.

as	has	fox	box	mix
egg	jam	pet	nap	big

1. A _____ was in the _____.

2. The hen has a _____ _____ in the nest.

3. Mom ate _____ on a bun.

4. Ned _____ to take a _____.

5. Can you _____ up the paint?

6. Ann has a _____ cat.

My Spelling Dictation

Write the sentences.
Circle the spelling words.

1. _____

_____

2. _____

_____

Circle the word in each row that has a different vowel sound.

1. jam   (box)   nap   has

2. pet   egg   mix   red

3. box   as   fox   got

4. it   mix   pet   rip

5. as   nap   big   has

Write the spelling words that rhyme.

| as | big | box | egg |
| nap | jam | mix | pet |

1. fox _____

2. has _____

3. get _____

4. pig _____

5. fix _____

6. ham _____

Spelling List

This Week's Focus:
- Spell short **i** and short **a** words
- Spell words in the **-all** and **-and** families

STEP 1 Read and Spell	STEP 2 Copy and Spell	STEP 3 Cover and Spell

fold

1. his

2. is

3. an

4. and

5. can

6. all

7. call

8. land

9. hand

10. small

11. _____
    bonus word

12. _____
    bonus word

Visual Memory

Fill in the boxes.

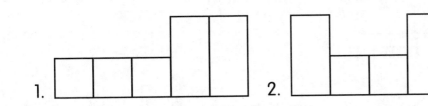

his   is   an   and   can

all   call   land   hand   small

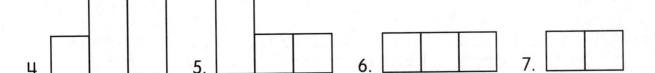

1.   2.   3.

4.   5.   6.   7.

8.   9.   10.

Spell Correctly

Unscramble the letters.

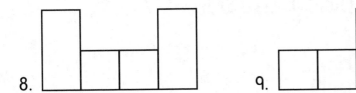

na _____   allsm _____   nac _____

si _____   nad _____   nahd _____

llac _____   shi _____   lal _____

andl _____   lacl _____   ladn _____

Word Meaning

Write the missing word on the line.

1. Mom put the cake in a _____ box.
   call, small, ball

2. I cut my _____.
   land, and, hand

3. Did the bug _____ on Kim's leg?
   and, land, hand

4. Pat must _____ his mom.
   small, tall, call

5. Put _____ the pigs in the pen.
   all, small, call

6. Is that _____ ball?
   is, and, his

My Spelling Dictation

Write the sentences.
Circle the spelling words.

1. _____

   _____

2. _____

   _____

14

Word Study

Read the words. Listen for the sounds of **a**.
Write each word in the correct box.

can	cat	small	and
fawn	call	want	has
land	saw	hand	ball

the sound of **a** in **an**	the sound of **a** in **all**
<u>can</u> _____	_____ _____
_____ _____	_____ _____
_____ _____	_____ _____
_____ _____	_____ _____

Complete each rhyme with a spelling word.

1. Raise your left <u>hand</u>

   if you see _____.

2. Throw the <u>ball</u>

   when I _____.

3. Please hand <u>Dan</u>

   the green _____.

4. <u>Is</u> this

   pig _____?

     Building Spelling Skills, Daily Practice • EMC 6682

Spelling List

This Week's Focus:
- Spell short vowel words
- Spell words with **or**
- Recognize homophones **four** and **for**
- Recognize the words **I** and **we**

STEP 1 Read and Spell

STEP 2 Copy and Spell

STEP 3 Cover and Spell

fold

1. up

2. it

3. him

4. I

5. for

6. or

7. four

8. we

9. man

10. men

11. _____
   bonus word

12. _____
   bonus word

Visual Memory

Fill in the boxes.

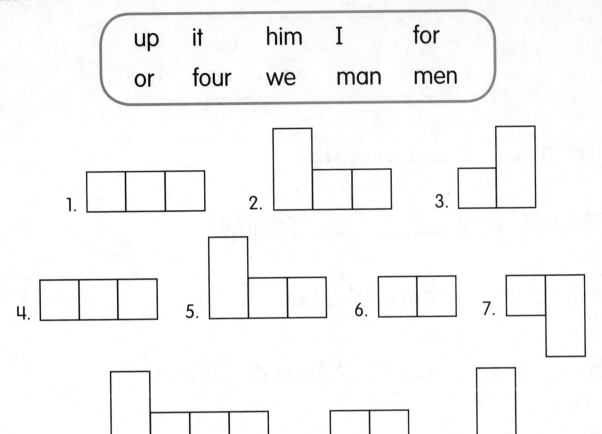

up   it   him   I   for
or   four   we   man   men

1.
2.
3.
4.
5.
6.
7.
8.
9.
10.

Find the Mistakes

Circle the words that are misspelled.

1. Tim has for dogs.

2. That min had a hat.

3. Can wee go with them?

4. Is the cake four me?

5. Did Nina see hem?

Word Meaning

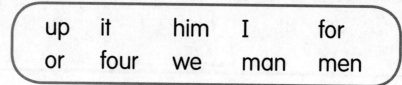

Fill in the missing word.

up	it	him	I	for
or	four	we	man	men

1. I want _____ cookies.

2. The red cap is _____ Tammy.

3. A _____ got on the bus.

4. Four _____ got off the bus.

5. Jose and _____ went to the zoo.

6. An ape climbed _____ in the tree.

My Spelling Dictation

Write the sentences.
Circle the spelling words.

1. _____

_____

2. _____

_____

Word Study

Add a letter to make a new word.

man	___an	___an
___en	**10** ___en	___en
___oat	___oat	___oat

Write the correct word on each line. Write **four** or **for**.

1. I will get it _____ you.

2. The _____ men lifted the box.

3. The little hen laid the egg _____ you.

4. The goat ate _____ bags of corn.

Spelling List

This Week's Focus:
- Review short vowel words
- Spell long vowel words with silent **e**

STEP 1 — Read and Spell

1. add
2. ask
3. came
4. name
5. ride
6. bone
7. save
8. kite
9. cute
10. mine
11. _____ bonus word
12. _____ bonus word

STEP 2 — Copy and Spell

STEP 3 — Cover and Spell

fold

Fill in the boxes.

add   ask   came   name   ride
bone   save   kite   cute   mine

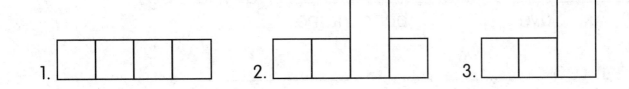

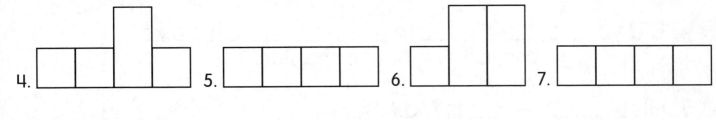

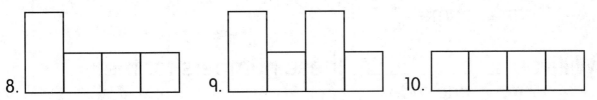

1.   2.   3.

4.   5.   6.   7.

8.   9.   10.

Find the Correct Word

Circle the word that is spelled correctly.

1. kame	came		6. bone	bown
2. ask	aks		7. myne	mine
3. kite	kyte		8. add	adde
4. ridd	ride		9. zave	save
5. qute	cute		10. name	naim

Building Spelling Skills, Daily Practice • EMC 6682

Word Meaning

Write the missing words on the lines.

1. The _____ kitten jumped on the bed.
   mine, cute

2. _____ that _____ for the dog.
   Ask, Save   bone, name

3. That red _____ is _____.
   save, kite   mine, add

4. Did you _____ to _____ his bike?
   add, ask   came, ride

5. His _____ is Max.
   came, name

6. Will you _____ these numbers for me?
   add, ride

7. John _____ to the birthday party.
   save, came

My Spelling Dictation

Write the sentences.
Circle the spelling words.

1. _____

   _____

2. _____

   _____

22

Word Study

Read the words. Listen for the vowel sounds.
Write each word in the correct box.

add	came	ride	up
save	him	men	cute
ask	bone	can	name
got	hand	mine	kite

long vowel sounds	short vowel sounds
_____ _____	_____ _____
_____ _____	_____ _____
_____ _____	_____ _____
_____ _____	_____ _____

Complete each rhyme with a spelling word.

1. Please ask your <u>Dad</u>

   how much to _____.

2. Does this <u>game</u>

   have a _____?

3. I will hold your <u>line</u>

   if you hold _____.

4. The dog is <u>alone</u>

   with his big _____.

Spelling List

This Week's Focus:
- Spell words with the long **e** sound spelled **e** or **ee**
- Spell short **o** words

STEP 1 Read and Spell

STEP 2 Copy and Spell

STEP 3 Cover and Spell

fold

1. be

2. see

3. got

4. she

5. sheep

6. shop

7. queen

8. green

9. bee

10. he

11. _____
   bonus word

12. _____
   bonus word

Visual Memory

Fill in the boxes.

be   see   he   she   sheep
bee   shop   queen   green   got

1.
2.
3.
4.
5.
6.
7.
8.
9.
10.

Spell Vowel Sounds

What is missing? Write **e** or **ee**.

 qu___n

 sh___p

 b___

1. s_ee_

2. h___

3. gr___n

4. b___

5. sh___

6. p___p

Fill in the missing words.

she	sheep	shop	queen
see	he	green	bee

1. The _____ has three white _____.

2. _____ keeps the sheep in a pen.

3. The queen got them at a _____.

4. Jim saw a _____ leaf.

5. A big _____ sat on a red bud.

6. Did _____ _____ the bee?

My Spelling Dictation

Write the sentences.
Circle the spelling words.

1. _____

_____

2. _____

_____

Word Study

Read the words. Listen for the sounds of **e**.
Write each word in the correct box.

be	get	see	queen
hen	mess	she	sheep
bell	bee	red	then

the sound of **e** in **me**	the sound of **e** in **pet**
_____ _____	_____ _____
_____ _____	_____ _____
_____ _____	_____ _____
_____ _____	_____ _____

Complete each rhyme with a spelling word.

1. Can you <u>see</u>

   the big _____?

2. Have you <u>seen</u>

   our fair _____?

3. We'll take the <u>jeep</u>

   to find the _____.

4. I bought the <u>top</u>

   at the toy _____.

Spelling List

This Week's Focus:
- Spell long **o** and long **a** words
- Recognize the vowel sound in **do**
- Spell words in the **-ind** family
- Add the ending **-ing** with no change to the base word

STEP 1 Read and Spell	STEP 2 Copy and Spell	STEP 3 Cover and Spell

fold

1. no

2. go

3. going

4. most

5. kind

6. find

7. gave

8. so

9. do

10. doing

11. _____
   bonus word

12. _____
   bonus word

Visual Memory

Fill in the boxes.

no	go	going	most	so
do	doing	kind	find	gave

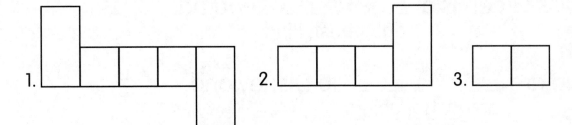

1. 2. 3.

4. 5. 6. 7.

8. 9. 10.

Make New Words

Change a letter to make a word.

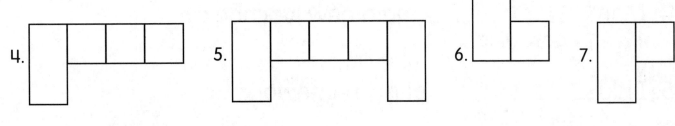

no   __g__o   cave   ____ave

mind   ____ind   post   ____ost

Add the ending **ing**.

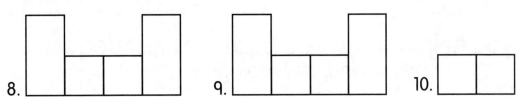

go   ____going____   find _____

do _____   sleep _____

Word Meaning

Write the missing word on the line.

1. What is that man _____?

2. Miss Green is a _____ woman.

3. We are _____ to Disneyland.

4. Mom _____ me a new lunchbox.

5. I did _____ of my homework.

6. Can you help me _____ my lost dog?

7. Tonya needs to _____ home now.

My Spelling Dictation

Circle the spelling words.

1. _____

2. _____

Word Study

Read the words. Listen for the vowel sounds.
Write each word in the correct box.

kind	gave	most	cake
do	to	so	find
save	go	mine	blue

sound of **o** in **no**	sound of **i** in **time**	sound of **a** in **cave**	sound of **o** in **too**
_____	_____	_____	_____
_____	_____	_____	_____
_____	_____	_____	_____
_____	_____	_____	_____

Fill in the blank to complete each **-ind** word.

1. I need to ____ind my watch.

2. You must ____ind the key.

3. What ____ind of bee is it?

4. He is a ____ind person.

Spelling List

This Week's Focus:
- Review long and short vowel words
- Spell words with the consonant digraph **th**
- Recognize the short **u** sound in **was** and **of**
- Recognize the vowel sound in **a**

STEP 1 Read and Spell   **STEP 2** Copy and Spell   **STEP 3** Cover and Spell

fold

1. the

2. that

3. them

4. day

5. may

6. made

7. was

8. of

9. if

10. a

11. _____
    bonus word

12. _____
    bonus word

Visual Memory

Fill in the boxes.

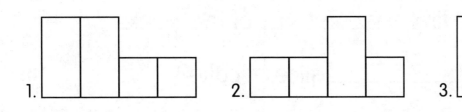

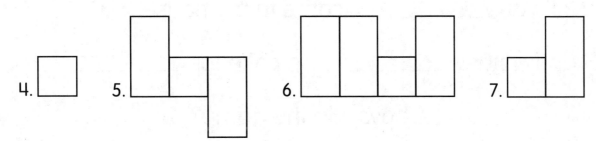

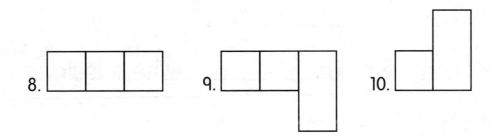

Find the Correct Word

Circle the word that is spelled correctly.

1. taht   that   4. wus   was

2. may   mai   5. dae   day

3. the   thu   6. them   thm

Fill in the missing words.

day	of	them	if	a
that	was	made	the	may

1. Sunday is the first _____ of the week.

2. May I have _____ slice of cake?

3. Ask if you _____ come to my house.

4. Grandmother _____ a cake for _____.

5. Will _____ boys win the game?

6. What is in _____ big box?

7. Bob will come with us _____ he has time.

8. The little boy's balloon _____ red.

My Spelling Dictation

Write the sentences.
Circle the spelling words.

1. _____

_____

2. _____

_____

Word Study

Read the words. Listen for the sounds of **a**.
Write each word in the correct box.

| may | sat | sand | made | game | flat |
| pan | cake | play | that | plant | stay |

short **a** sound	long **a** sound
_____ _____	_____ _____
_____ _____	_____ _____
_____ _____	_____ _____
_____ _____	_____ _____

Say the word aloud. Circle the letters that stand for the first sound you hear.

the   them   that

Use these words to fill in the blanks.

the   them   that

1. May I go with _____?

2. _____ is a big dog!

3. I am not in _____ house.

Spelling List

This Week's Focus:
- Review short **u**, long **u**, and long **o** words
- Recognize the short **u** sound in **some** and **come**
- Add the ending -**ing** after doubling the final consonant

STEP 1 Read and Spell

STEP 2 Copy and Spell

STEP 3 Cover and Spell

fold

1. some

2. come

3. home

4. fun

5. funny

6. run

7. running

8. ran

9. us

10. use

11. _____
       bonus word

12. _____
       bonus word

Visual Memory

Fill in the boxes.

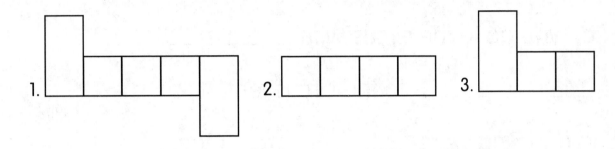

some   come   home   fun   funny

ran   run   use   us   running

1.

2.

3.

4.

5.

6.

7.

8.

9.

10.

Making New Words

Write the last letter a second time.
Then add **ing** to the word.

1. run   __running__

2. hit   _____

3. hum   _____

4. tag   _____

5. cut   _____

6. tap   _____

7. rub   _____

8. sit   _____

Fill in the missing word.

some	come	home	fun	funny
ran	run	use	us	running

1. Can you go to the circus with _____?

2. I _____ to the circus tent.

3. Sid and Tina were _____, too.

4. Will the clowns _____ here?

5. The _____ clowns jumped up and down.

6. _____ clowns were in a little car.

7. We had _____ at the circus.

8. It is time to go _____.

My Spelling Dictation

Write the sentences.
Circle the spelling words.

1. _____

_____

2. _____

_____

Word Study

Read the words. Listen for the vowel sounds.
Write each word in the correct box.

some	home	stone	fun
come	bone	don't	jump
joke	run	us	boat

the sound of **u** in **up**	the sound of **o** in **no**
_____ _____	_____ _____
_____ _____	_____ _____
_____ _____	_____ _____
_____ _____	_____ _____

Fill in each blank with the correct word.

ran   run   running

1. I _____ to meet the train this morning.

2. I like to _____ on the grass.

3. He is _____ in a big race today.

Spelling List

This Week's Focus:
- Review long **a** and long **i** words
- Spell the vowel sounds in **help**, **here**, and **want**
- Add the ending **-ing** after dropping the silent **e**
- Recognize homophones

| STEP 1 Read and Spell | STEP 2 Copy and Spell | STEP 3 Cover and Spell |

fold

1. place

2. make

3. making

4. help

5. here

6. want

7. nice

8. to

9. two

10. into

11. _____
   bonus word

12. _____
   bonus word

Visual Memory

Fill in the boxes.

place	make	help	here	want
nice	to	two	into	making

1.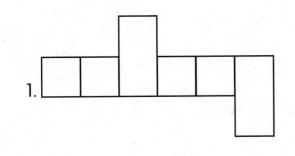

2.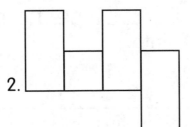

3.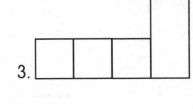

4.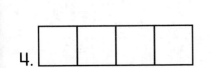

5.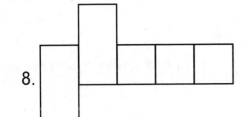

6.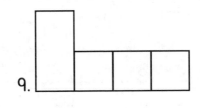

7.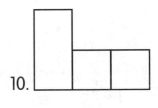

8.

9.

10.

Find the Mistakes

Mark an **X** on the misspelled words.

1. hep   help
2. make   mak
3. intwo   into
4. nize   nice
5. place   plaic

6. makking   making
7. twe   two
8. here   heer
9. wunt   want
10. to   tou

Word Meaning

Write the missing words on the lines.

1. Can you _____ me _____ a cake?
   here, help   making, make

2. That is a _____ pet hamster.
   nice, into

3. I _____ _____ cookies.
   want, to   two, make

4. Let's go _____ the mall.
   two, to

5. Toss the ball _____ the hoop.
   into, two

6. _____ is the _____ to get ice cream.
   Help, Here   place, make

My Spelling Dictation

Write the sentences.
Circle the spelling words.

1. _____

   _____

2. _____

   _____

42

Word Study

Make a new word by adding **ing**.
Be sure to follow the rules.

> • Just add **ing**
>   play + ing = playing
> • Drop silent **e** and then add **ing**
>   mak~~e~~ + ing = making

1. bake _baking_

2. want _____

3. sing _____

4. ride _____

5. take _____

6. start _____

7. wash _____

8. come _____

9. chase _____

10. smile _____

Fill in the missing word.

1. Mom is _____ cookies today.
   bake, baking

2. I will _____ the glass on the table.
   place, placing

3. You are _____ a pretty picture.
   make, making

4. He must _____ the bus to work.
   take, taking

Building Spelling Skills, Daily Practice • EMC 6682

Spelling List

This Week's Focus:
- Spell words with the final consonant blends **nd** and **st**
- Spell words with the final consonant digraph **th**
- Spell words with the /**k**/ sound spelled **ck**

STEP 1 Read and Spell

STEP 2 Copy and Spell

STEP 3 Cover and Spell

fold

1. send

2. pick

3. end

4. both

5. fast

6. last

7. must

8. just

9. bath

10. black

11. _____
   bonus word

12. _____
   bonus word

Visual Memory

Fill in the boxes.

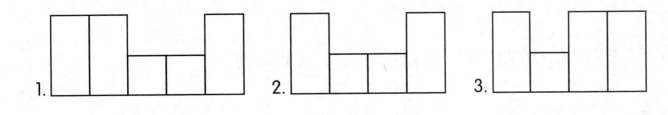

send   pick   end   both   fast

last   must   just   bath   black

1.   2.   3.

4.   5.   6.   7.

8.   9.   10.

Rhyming Words

Write the words that rhyme.

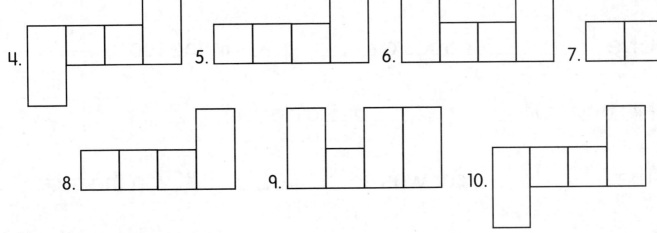

just   cast   trick   last   kick   past

send   sick   dust   mend   rust   bend

pick	**end**	**fast**	**must**
trick			

Building Spelling Skills, Daily Practice • EMC 6682

Fill in the missing words.

send	pick	end	both	fast
last	must	just	bath	black

1. The ballgame will _____ all day.

2. I was happy to _____ my prize.

3. Give _____ dogs a _____ in the tub.

4. His party will _____ at 5 o'clock.

5. The _____ car was so _____ it won the race.

6. Will Uncle Fred _____ me a letter?

My Spelling Dictation

Write the sentences.
Circle the spelling words.

1. _____

   _____

2. _____

   _____

Word Study

Add an ending to make a word. Write **th**, **st**, **ck**, or **nd**.

ba_____	sa_____	mo_____
chi_____	bla_____	ba_____

Fill in the missing letters.

1. Put the bla_____ chi_____ in the pen with the hen.

2. He mu_____ go home soon.

3. Did you take a ba_____?

4. I mu_____ run fa_____ or I will come in la_____.

47 Building Spelling Skills, Daily Practice • EMC 6682

Spelling List

This Week's Focus:

- Spell words with the long **i** or long **e** sound spelled **y**
- Review short and long vowel spelling patterns
- Study contractions

STEP 1 Read and Spell

STEP 2 Copy and Spell

STEP 3 Cover and Spell

fold

1. candy

2. went

3. sent

4. take

5. like

6. puppy

7. time

8. didn't

9. by

10. my

11. _____
   bonus word

12. _____
   bonus word

Visual Memory

Fill in the boxes.

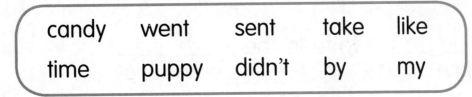

candy   went   sent   take   like

time   puppy   didn't   by   my

1.
2.
3.
4.
5.
6.
7.
8.
9.
10.

Contractions

Match the contractions to the correct words.

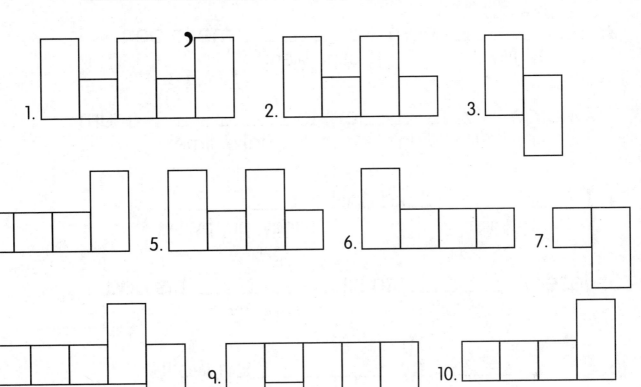

didn't	is not
can't	did not
isn't	cannot
I'm	it is
let's	I am
it's	let us

Word Meaning

Write the missing words on the lines.

1. It's _____ to feed the _____.
    time, like   sent, puppy

2. _____ mom _____ me to bed.
    By, My   sent, went

3. George _____ get to _____ a turn.
         like, didn't   take, time

4. I _____ cake and _____.
      take, like   candy, puppy

5. Jose _____ to sit _____ his dad.
         my, went   sent, by

6. I _____ my _____ on walks.
      didn't, take   by, puppy

My Spelling Dictation

Write the sentences.
Circle the spelling words.

1. _____

_____

2. _____

_____

Word Study

Read the words. Listen for the sounds of **y**.
Write each word in the correct box.

candy	by	your	funny
my	happy	yell	try
yam	yes	fly	puppy

sound of **y** in **sunny**	sound of **y** in **cry**	sound of **y** in **you**

Complete each rhyme with a spelling word.

1. Ask <u>Mandy</u>

   for some _____.

2. Where is the <u>tent</u>

   you were _____?

3. If you give me a <u>dime</u>

   I will tell you the _____.

4. Which racing <u>bike</u>

   do you really _____?

Spelling List

This Week's Focus:
- Practice spelling words with double consonants
- Distinguish between one- and two-syllable words

STEP 1 Read and Spell

STEP 2 Copy and Spell

STEP 3 Cover and Spell

fold

1. less

2. tell

3. well

4. will

5. still

6. off

7. letter

8. little

9. silly

10. happy

11. _____
bonus word

12. _____
bonus word

Fill in the boxes.

| less | tell | will | still | letter |
| little | off | well | silly | happy |

1.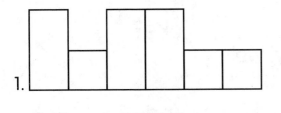

2.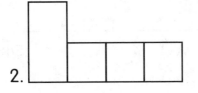

3.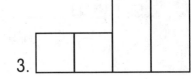

4.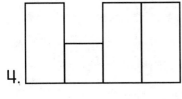

5.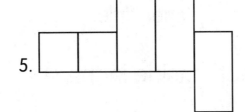

6.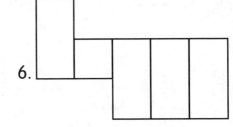

7.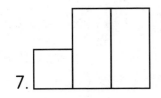

8.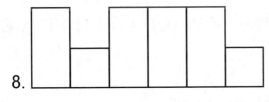

9.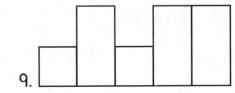

10.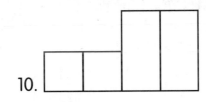

Find the Mistakes

Mark an **X** on the misspelled words.

1. wil   will
2. hapy   happy
3. letter   leter
4. off   oof
5. sily   silly

6. less   les
7. litle   little
8. tel   tell
9. well   wel
10. still   stell

Write the missing words on the lines.

1. Mom was _____ to get a _____ from Grandma.
   little, happy   letter, less

2. Can you _____ me a _____ joke?
   tell, will   silly, well

3. I _____ take a _____ bit of candy.
   well, will   letter, little

4. It is _____ hot outside in the sun.
   will, still

5. Turn _____ the TV when you go to bed.
   little, off

6. Is six _____ than ten?
   less, tell

My Spelling Dictation

Write the sentences.
Circle the spelling words.

1. _____

   _____

2. _____

   _____

Word Study

Write the words that rhyme.

better	dress	four	seen
some	well	when	will

1. less   _____

2. tell   _____

3. still   _____

4. letter   _____

5. come   _____

6. or   _____

7. men   _____

8. queen   _____

Circle the number of syllables in each word.

1. letter   1   2

2. silly   1   2

3. well   1   2

4. less   1   2

5. little   1   2

6. happy   1   2

7. still   1   2

8. rabbit   1   2

9. bunny   1   2

10. black   1   2

11. into   1   2

12. two   1   2

13. lasted   1   2

14. place   1   2

15. help   1   2

16. making   1   2

Building Spelling Skills

WEEK 14

Spelling List

This Week's Focus:
- Spell words in the **-oat**, **-ong**, and **-all** families
- Spell words with the vowel digraph **aw**

STEP 1 Read and Spell	STEP 2 Copy and Spell	STEP 3 Cover and Spell

(fold)

1. boat

2. coat

3. float

4. long

5. along

6. belong

7. paw

8. fawn

9. tall

10. wall

11. _____
bonus word

12. _____
bonus word

Visual Memory

Fill in the boxes.

boat   float   coat   long   along
belong   paw   fawn   tall   wall

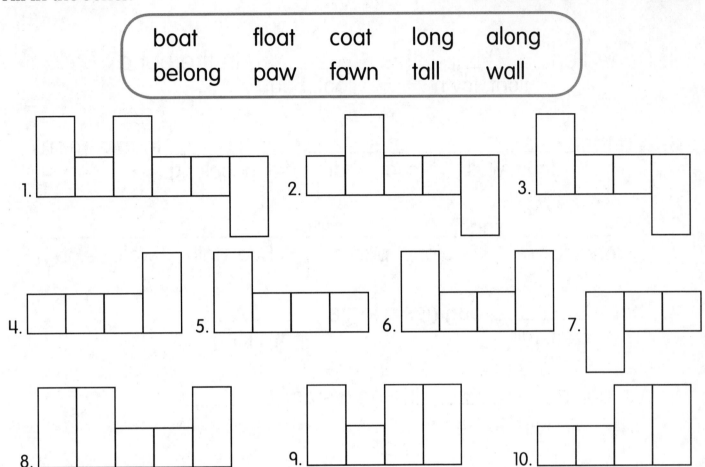

1.
2.
3.
4.
5.
6.
7.
8.
9.
10.

Spell Vowel Sounds

Add the missing letters. Write **aw**, **all**, or **oa**.

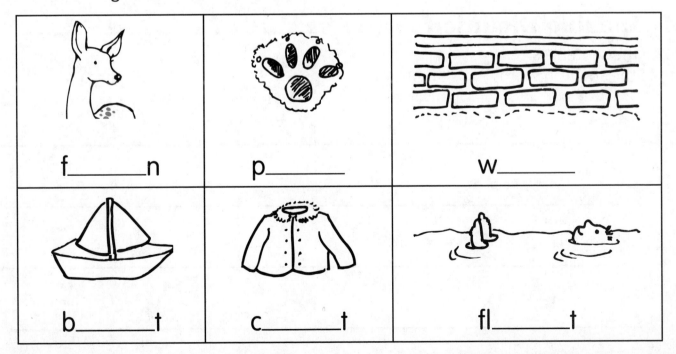

f_____n   p_____   w_____

b_____t   c____t   fl_____t

Word Meaning

Write the missing words on the lines.

1. Can Allen _____ his _____ in the pond?
   float, fawn   coat, boat

2. Did the _____ _____ _____ to that man?
   long, wall   coat, float   along, belong

3. A _____ ran _____ the _____ _____.
   long, fawn   along, paw   boat, tall   wall, belong

4. The _____ dog has a large _____.
   coat, tall   paw, long

5. We took a _____ trip on a small _____.
   long, float   boat, fawn

6. The stone _____ runs _____ the road.
   boat, wall   belong, along

My Spelling Dictation

Write the sentences.
Circle the spelling words.

1. _____

   _____

2. _____

   _____

Word Study

Read the words. Listen for rhyming words.
Write each word in the correct box.

boat	tall	coat	call	float
along	long	belong	wall	

-all	-ong	-oat
call		

Complete each rhyme with a spelling word.

1. We will <u>float</u>

   in the _____.

2. At <u>dawn</u>

   we saw a _____.

3. The ball will <u>fall</u>

   from the tall _____.

4. We think we <u>belong</u>

   where the river is _____.

59   Building Spelling Skills, Daily Practice • EMC 6682

Spelling List

This Week's Focus:
- Spell words with the vowel digraphs **ai** and **ay**
- Review long **a** words with silent **e**

STEP 1 Read and Spell

STEP 2 Copy and Spell

STEP 3 Cover and Spell

fold

1. way
2. away
3. today
4. chain
5. wait
6. chase
7. play
8. played
9. rain
10. paint
11. _____ bonus word
12. _____ bonus word

Visual Memory

Fill in the boxes.

> way   away   today   play   played
>
> chain   chase   paint   wait   rain

1.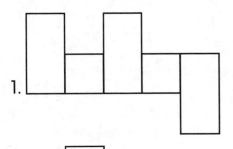

2.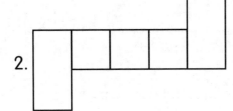

3.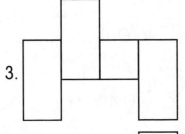

4.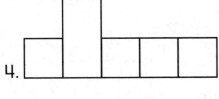

5.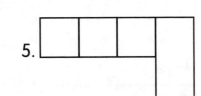

6.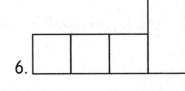

7.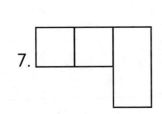

8.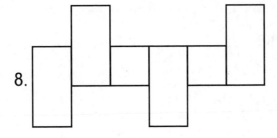

9.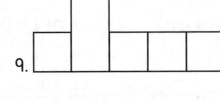

10.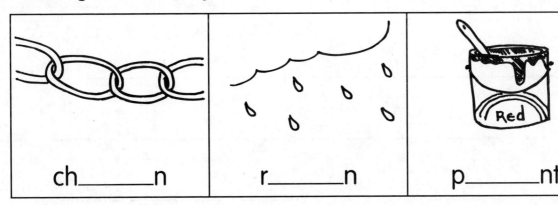

Spell Vowel Sounds

What is missing? Write **ai** or **ay**.

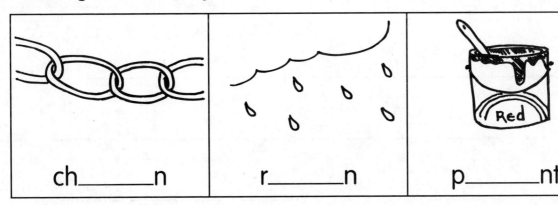

ch____n   r____n   p____nt

w_____   w_____t   pl_____   tod_____

Word Meaning

Fill in the missing words.

way	away	today	play	played
chain	chase	paint	wait	rain

1. We like to _____ kickball.

2. Don't run _____!

3. Did Arnold's dog _____ the cat?

4. We are going to _____ the gate _____.

5. Carlos got wet in the _____.

6. Lock up your bike with that _____.

My Spelling Dictation

Write the sentences.
Circle the spelling words.

1. _____

_____

2. _____

_____

Read the words. Listen for rhyming words.
Write each word in the correct box.

chain	way	chase	rain	play
case	face	away	today	pain
lane	race	main	stay	place

say	gain	vase
way		

Write a rhyming spelling word.

1. bay

_____

2. bait

_____

3. stayed

_____

4. faint

_____

5. vase

_____

6. rain

_____

Building Spelling Skills, Daily Practice • EMC 6682

Spelling List

This Week's Focus:
- Spell words with the vowel digraph **oo**
- Recognize the two sounds of **oo**
- Spell words with the initial consonant digraph **wh**

STEP 1 Read and Spell

STEP 2 Copy and Spell

STEP 3 Cover and Spell

fold

1. too

2. good

3. book

4. shook

5. school

6. when

7. what

8. took

9. who

10. soon

11. _____
   bonus word

12. _____
   bonus word

Visual Memory

Fill in the boxes.

too	good	book	shook	school
soon	what	when	who	took

1.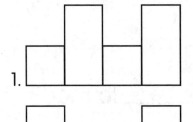

2.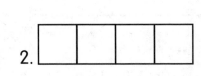

3.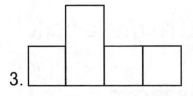

4.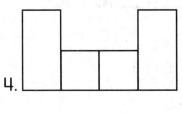

5.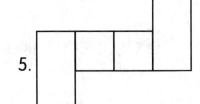

6.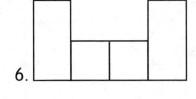

7.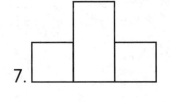

8.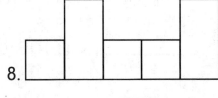

9.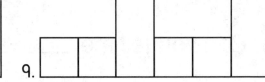

10.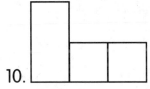

Find the Correct Word

Circle the words that are spelled correctly.

1. skool   school

2. good   gud

3. shook   shoock

4. whoo   who

5. took   twok

6. wat   what

7. when   wen

8. bock   book

Word Meaning

Fill in the missing words.

too	good	book	shook	school
soon	what	when	who	took

1. It's time to go to _____.

2. Is that a _____ _____ to read?

3. He _____ the bell to make it ring.

4. _____ tore this book?

5. Can you tell me _____ is in the box?

6. Zeke wants to go swimming, _____.

My Spelling Dictation

Write the sentences.
Circle the spelling words.

1. _____

_____

2. _____

_____

Building Spelling Skills WEEK **16**

Read the words. Listen for the sounds of **oo**.
Write each word in the correct box.

school	good	cook	soon
shook	too	hook	took
boo	look	tool	who

sound of **oo** in **too**	sound of **oo** in **book**
<u>boo</u> _____	_____ _____
_____ _____	_____ _____
_____ _____	_____ _____
_____ _____	_____ _____

Complete each rhyme with a spelling word.

1. The red <u>hood</u>

   looks very _____.

2. My teacher <u>took</u>

   the last _____.

3. The full <u>moon</u>

   will shine _____.

4. Will you <u>look</u>

   at what he _____?

Spelling List

This Week's Focus:
- Spell words with the vowel digraphs **ow** and **ou**
- Recognize the two sounds of **ow**

STEP 1 Read and Spell

STEP 2 Copy and Spell

STEP 3 Cover and Spell

fold

1. now

2. down

3. how

4. out

5. shout

6. about

7. our

8. house

9. slow

10. show

11. _____
   bonus word

12. _____
   bonus word

Visual Memory

Fill in the boxes.

| now | down | how | out | shout |
| about | our | house | slow | show |

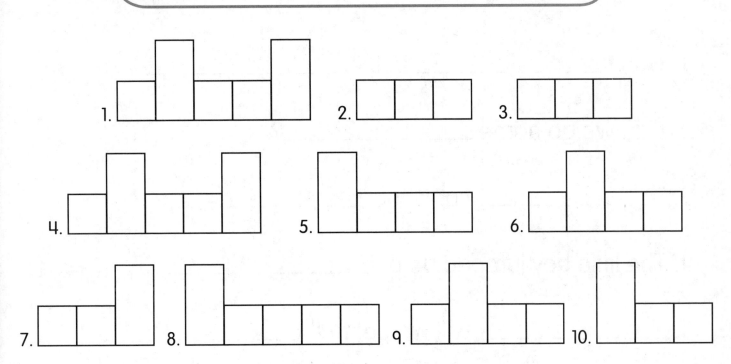

Spell Vowel Sounds

What is missing? Write **ow** or **ou**.

1. h_ OU _se   5. _____t   9. h_____

2. sh_____   6. n_____   10. _____r

3. d_____n   7. ab_____t   11. sh_____

4. sh_____t   8. sl_____   12. cl_____n

Fill in the missing words.

> now   down   how   out   shout
>
> about   our   house   slow   show

1. Don't _____ in the _____.

2. Can we go home _____?

3. _____ car is too _____.

4. The little boy jumped up and _____.

5. _____ will we get to the _____?

6. This book is _____ dinosaurs.

My Spelling Dictation

Write the sentences.
Circle the spelling words.

1. _____

_____

2. _____

_____

Word Study

Read the words. Listen for the vowel sounds.
Write each word in the correct box.

show	now	row	out	grow
our	go	down	how	shout
mow	about	bone	slow	house

sound of **ow** in **cow**	sound of **o** in **no**
_____ _____	_____ _____
_____ _____	_____ _____
_____ _____	_____ _____
_____ _____	_____ _____

Write a rhyming spelling word.

1. cow _____   4. town _____

2. shout _____   5. sour _____

3. mouse _____   6. show _____

Spelling List

This Week's Focus:
- Spell words with r-controlled vowels spelled **er**, **ir**, **ur**, and **ar**

STEP 1 Read and Spell

STEP 2 Copy and Spell

STEP 3 Cover and Spell

fold

1. her

2. girl

3. turn

4. hurt

5. first

6. were

7. card

8. part

9. start

10. are

11. _____
    bonus word

12. _____
    bonus word

Visual Memory

Fill in the boxes.

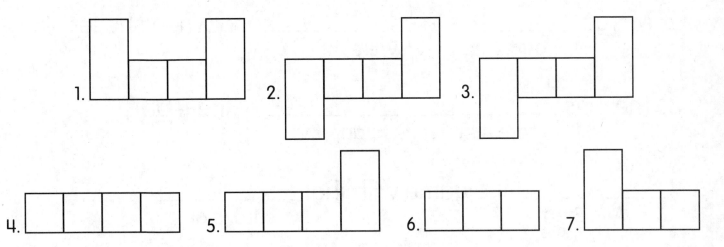

her	girl	turn	hurt	first
were	card	part	start	are

1.

2.

3.

4.

5.

6.

7.

8.

9.

10.

Find the Mistakes

Mark an **X** on the misspelled words.

1. That gril hurt her leg.

2. Did the game stard?

3. The ferst joke was funny.

4. It is Bob's tirn next.

Word Meaning

Write the missing words on the lines.

1. She was the _____ _____ to play ball.

her, first   hurt, girl

2. Margo _____ _____ hand when she fell.

part, hurt   were, her

3. The girls _____ _____ of the team.

are, turn   start, part

4. _____ the game with that _____.

Are, Start   card, start

5. The next _____ is Kelly's.

turn, were

6. Where _____ you yesterday?

hurt, were

My Spelling Dictation

Write the sentences.
Circle the spelling words.

1. _____

_____

2. _____

_____

Write the letters that spell the /**er**/ sound in the words.

> er   ir   ur

1. h_____

2. t_____n

3. g_____l

4. h_____t

5. w_____e

6. f_____st

7. st_____

8. c_____l

9. t_____key

10. n_____se

Find the Correct Word

Circle the words that are spelled correctly.

1. ar	are		6. gurl	girl
2. card	kard		7. turn	tern
3. strat	start		8. furs	first
4. part	pard		9. wer	were
5. her	hur		10. hurt	hert

Spelling List

This Week's Focus:
- Spell words with initial consonant blends **fl**, **bl**, and **st**
- Spell words in the **-ore**, **-ew**, and **-ing** families

STEP 1 Read and Spell	STEP 2 Copy and Spell	STEP 3 Cover and Spell

fold

1. more

2. store

3. stand

4. star

5. blew

6. flew

7. new

8. stone

9. sting

10. ring

11. _____
   bonus word

12. _____
   bonus word

Visual Memory

Fill in the boxes.

more	store	stand	star	blew
new	flew	stone	sting	ring

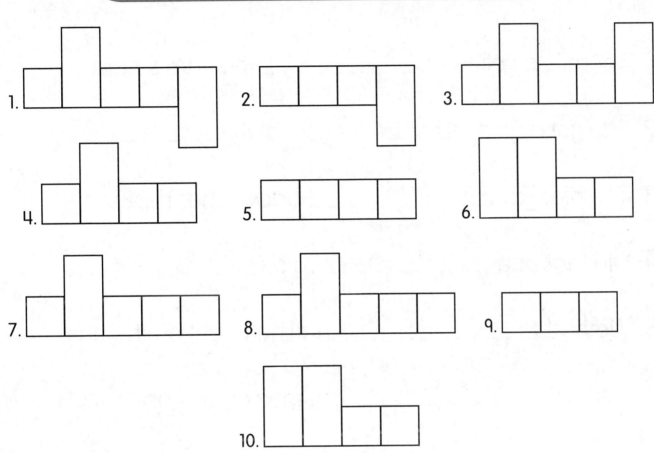

1.
2.
3.
4.
5.
6.
7.
8.
9.
10.

Find the Mistakes

Circle the misspelled words.

1. I went to the stor for Mom.

2. He blue up a red balloon.

3. The bird flu into a tree.

4. Did a bee styng Jamal?

5. Can I have some moor cookies?

Fill in the missing words.

more	store	stand	star	blew
new	flew	stone	sting	ring

1. There is a yellow _____ on Pam's hat.

2. She got a gold _____ at the _____.

3. The blue jay _____ back to her nest.

4. Did that bee _____ you?

5. We had to _____ in line to get on the bus.

6. Herman _____ out the candles on his cake.

My Spelling Dictation

Write the sentences.
Circle the spelling words.

1. _____

_____

2. _____

_____

Add the missing letters. Write **st**, **bl**, or **fl**.

_____ar

_____ocks

_____y

_____ackbird

_____ick

_____ag

Circle the letters that make the same /oo/ sound as in **too**.

flew	moon	school	tool
you	who	too	do
to	chew	tooth	new

Complete each rhyme with a spelling word.

1. Are there <u>more</u>

   at the _____?

2. The rich <u>king</u>

   has a _____.

Spelling List

This Week's Focus:
- Spell words ending in **ve**
- Spell words with the consonant blends **fr** and **ld**
- Spell words with the final consonant digraph **ch**
- Recognize the short **u** sound spelled **ove**

STEP 1 Read and Spell	STEP 2 Copy and Spell	STEP 3 Cover and Spell

fold

1. have

2. give

3. love

4. from

5. live

6. friend

7. much

8. such

9. old

10. told

11. _____
   bonus word

12. _____
   bonus word

Visual Memory

Fill in the boxes.

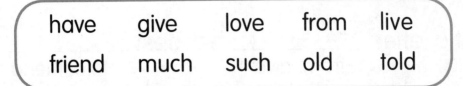

have	give	love	from	live
friend	much	such	old	told

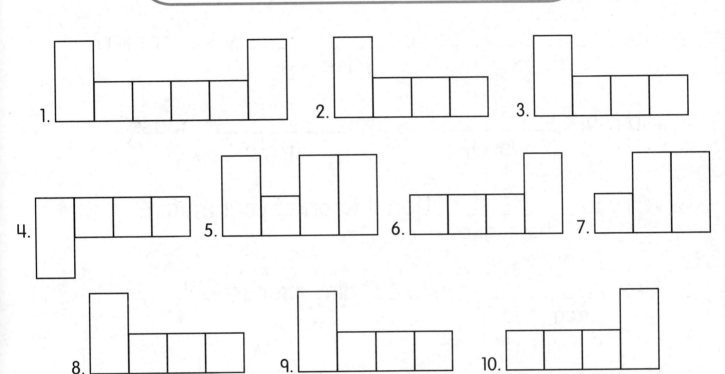

1.
2.
3.
4.
5.
6.
7.
8.
9.
10.

Rhyming Words

Match the words that rhyme.

give	such
old	live
much	glove
love	told
from	lend
friend	some

long	note
coat	some
too	song
rope	bunny
come	to
funny	soap

Building Spelling Skills, Daily Practice • EMC 6682

Word Meaning

Write the missing words on the lines.

1. She got a letter _____ her best _____.
   from, give   told, friend

2. How _____ do you _____ your mother?
   such, much   live, love

3. Did Mark _____ in that _____ house?
   live, give   have, old

4. Will you _____ Donald part of your muffin?
   have, give

5. Alex _____ me to call him after school.
   from, told

6. You _____ _____ a cute dog!
   have, told   much, such

My Spelling Dictation

Write the sentences.
Circle the spelling words.

1. _____

   _____

2. _____

   _____

Word Study

Read the words. Listen for the vowel sounds.
Write each word in the correct box.

stove	have	glove	gave
give	shove	five	wave
love	dive	save	above

long vowel sound	short vowel sound
_____ _____	_____ _____
_____ _____	_____ _____
_____ _____	_____ _____

Write a rhyming spelling word.

1. live
_____

2. dove
_____

3. some
_____

4. such
_____

5. bold
_____

Use words from above to complete the sentence.

I _____ to _____ my friends presents.

Building Spelling Skills, Daily Practice • EMC 6682

Spelling List

This Week's Focus:
- Spell words with the initial /**y**/ sound
- Review long **i** words with the silent **e**
- Spell words with the initial consonant blend **dr**
- Spell words with the vowel digraph **aw**

STEP 1 Read and Spell

STEP 2 Copy and Spell

STEP 3 Cover and Spell

fold

1. you

2. your

3. yes

4. yell

5. drop

6. line

7. side

8. dress

9. draw

10. saw

11. _____
   bonus word

12. _____
   bonus word

Fill in the boxes.

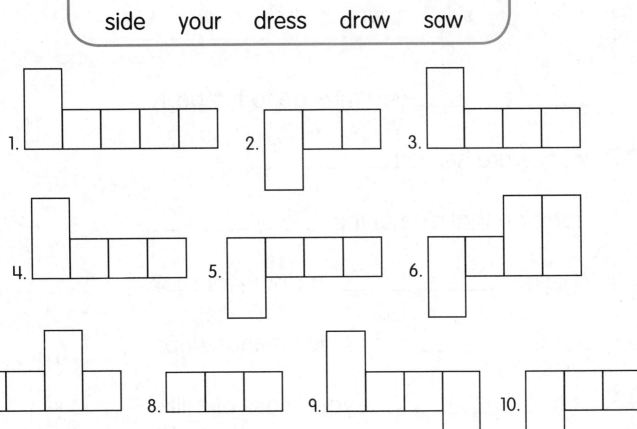

| you | yes | yell | drop | line |
| side | your | dress | draw | saw |

Find the Correct Word

Circle the word that is spelled correctly.

1. uoo   yeew   you

2. dess   dress   dreds

3. side   syde   sihd

4. zaw   saw   sah

5. grop   jrop   drop

6. line   yine   lin

Word Meaning

Fill in the missing word.

you	yes	yell	drop	line
side	your	dress	draw	saw

1. _____, you may go to the party.

2. Mary wore her red _____.

3. Stand on that side of the _____.

4. Will you _____ a clown for me?

5. Use the _____ to cut that wood.

6. Don't _____ your glass of milk.

7. I will _____ if you hit me.

My Spelling Dictation

Write the sentences.
Circle the spelling words.

1. _____

_____

2. _____

_____

Look at the pictures.
Fill in the missing letters. Write **tr**, **dr**, or **cr**.

_____uck	_____ess	_____ab
_____ee	_____own	_____um
_____icket	_____agon	_____umpet

Read the sentences.
Fill in the missing letters. Write **tr**, **dr**, or **cr**.

1. The baby began to _____y.

2. Throw that junk in the _____ash can.

3. Don't _____ip water on the clean floor.

4. The farmer planted a new _____op of corn.

5. We rode the _____ain to New York.

Spelling List

This Week's Focus:
- Spell words with diphthongs **oi** and **oy**
- Spell words that end with -**ther** or -**ter**
- Distinguish between one-, two-, and three-syllable words

STEP 1 Read and Spell

STEP 2 Copy and Spell

STEP 3 Cover and Spell

fold

1. boy

2. toy

3. oil

4. soil

5. other

6. mother

7. sister

8. boil

9. brother

10. father

11. _____
   bonus word

12. _____
   bonus word

Fill in the boxes.

> boy   toy   oil   soil   boil
>
> mother   father   sister   brother   other

1.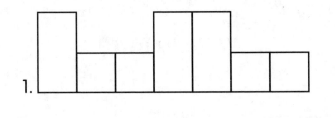

2.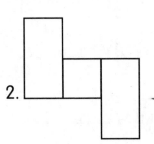

3.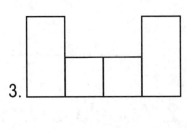

4.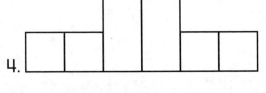

5.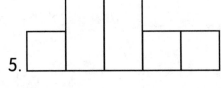

6.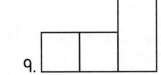

7.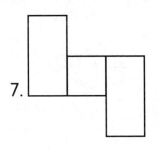

8.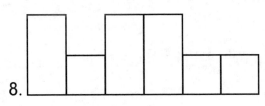

9.

10.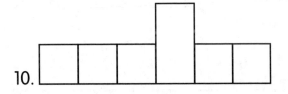

Word Study

What is missing? Write **oy** or **oi**.

1. b_____

2. b_____l

3. c_____n

4. R_____

5. s_____l

6. _____l

7. t_____

8. n_____se

Building Spelling Skills, Daily Practice • EMC 6682

Word Meaning

Fill in the missing words.

> boy   toy   oil   soil   boil
>
> mother   father   sister   brother   other

1. _____ and _____ went to town.

2. Angela is my baby _____.

3. Is that _____ your big _____?

4. The water will _____ when it gets very hot.

5. Jack likes this show, but I like the _____ one.

6. Plant seeds in the _____ in that pot.

My Spelling Dictation

Write the sentences.
Circle the spelling words.

1. _____

_____

2. _____

_____

Word Study

Change letters to make new words.

b	m	s	t	br

1. Roy   ____oy   ____oy

2. oil   ____oil   ____oil

3. other   ____other   ____other

4. twister   ____ister   ____ister

Circle the number of syllables in each word.

1. boy   1   2   3   5. mother   1   2   3

2. brother   1   2   3   6. family   1   2   3

3. sister   1   2   3   7. father   1   2   3

4. another   1   2   3   8. other   1   2   3

Complete each rhyme with a spelling word.

1. Don't put <u>oil</u>

   on the _____.

2. Ask the <u>boy</u>

   for a _____.

Spelling List

This Week's Focus:
- Spell words with final consonant digraphs **th** and **sh**
- Spell words with final consonant blends **ng** and **nk**

STEP 1 Read and Spell	STEP 2 Copy and Spell	STEP 3 Cover and Spell

fold

1. this

2. then

3. thing

4. thank

5. bank

6. with

7. wish

8. think

9. sing

10. these

11. _____
   bonus word

12. _____
   bonus word

Visual Memory

Fill in the boxes.

| this | then | these | thing | think |
| bank | with | thank | sing | wish |

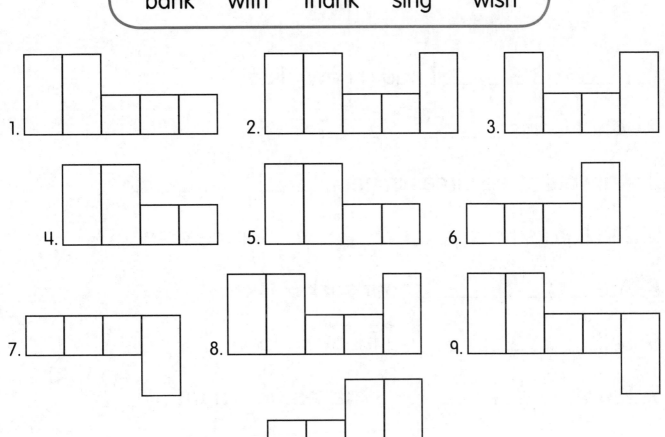

Final Sounds

Add ending letters to make words.

nk   ng   sh   th

1. thi_____   thi_____

2. wi_____   wi_____

   wi_____   wi_____

3. si_____   si_____

4. ba_____   ba_____

   ba_____   ba_____

Fill in the missing word.

> | this | then | these | thing | think |
> | bank | with | thank | sing | wish |

1. I _____ I had a new bike.

2. What is this _____?

3. Katy put three dimes in her _____.

4. Did Lara say _____ you for the present?

5. Are _____ your socks?

6. Let's _____ a funny song.

7. Did you _____ the test was hard?

8. Put the chicks in _____ the mother hen.

My Spelling Dictation

Write the sentences.
Circle the spelling words.

1. _____

_____

2. _____

_____

Write a rhyming spelling word.

1. blink _____   4. when _____

2. fish _____   5. miss _____

3. blank _____   6. ring _____

Listen for the /**th**/ and /**sh**/ sounds as you write the missing words on the lines.

1. _____ are good books.
   This, These

2. I got dressed and _____ went to school.
   then, this

3. You forgot one _____ on the test.
   think, thing

4. Did you say _____ you?
   thank, think

5. I _____ you could come for a visit.
   with, wish

6. May I go _____ you to the store?
   wish, with

7. Is _____ your kitten?
   these, this

Spelling List

This Week's Focus:
- Review words with the long **i** or long **e** sound spelled **y**
- Spell words with the long **e** sound spelled **ea**
- Spell words with initial blends **tr** and **fl**

STEP 1 Read and Spell

STEP 2 Copy and Spell

STEP 3 Cover and Spell

fold

1. why

2. try

3. trying

4. eat

5. mean

6. read

7. sunny

8. fly

9. treat

10. each

11. _____
    bonus word

12. _____
    bonus word

Visual Memory

Fill in the boxes.

> why   try   trying   fly   eat
> mean   each   read   treat   sunny

1.

2.

3.

4.

5.

6.

7.

8.

9.

10.

Beginning Sounds

Change letters to make new spelling words.

> r   m   s   fl   tr   cr   wh

1. fry   _____y

2. meat   _____eat

3. funny _____unny

4. bean   _____ean

5. bead   _____ead

6. shy   _____y

Word Meaning

Write the answers.

1. Name a treat you can eat.

_____

2. Name three things that can fly.

_____ _____ _____

3. What can you do on a sunny day?

_____

4. Name two things you can read.

_____ _____

5. What happens if you are mean to an animal?

_____

6. Circle the word that asks a question.

     try   why   fly

My Spelling Dictation

Write the sentences.
Circle the spelling words.

1. _____

   _____

2. _____

   _____

Word Study

Read the words. Listen for the vowel sounds.
Write each word in the correct box.

why	I	eat	see
time	treat	try	keep
mean	mine	read	pie
fly	each	bike	me

long **i**	long **e**
_____ _____	_____ _____
_____ _____	_____ _____
_____ _____	_____ _____
_____ _____	_____ _____

Complete each rhyme with a spelling word.

1. What may I <u>eat</u>

   as a small _____?

2. The baby bird will <u>try</u>

   his very best to _____.

3. The funny <u>bunny</u>

   likes when it is _____.

4. Will you <u>lead</u>

   when I _____?

Spelling List

This Week's Focus:
- Spell words with initial consonant blends **tr** and **st**
- Add the ending **-ed** after doubling the final consonant
- Spell **say** and **said**
- Spell words with the short **u** sound

STEP 1 Read and Spell

STEP 2 Copy and Spell

STEP 3 Cover and Spell

fold

1. trip
2. tree
3. say
4. said
5. hop
6. train
7. number
8. stop
9. stopped
10. one
11. _____ bonus word
12. _____ bonus word

Visual Memory

Fill in the boxes.

trip	say	tree	train	number
hop	said	stop	one	stopped

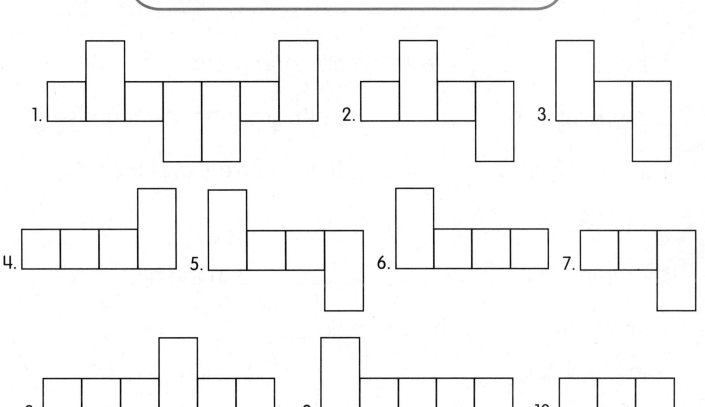

Rhyming Words

Match the words that rhyme.

say   skip

trip   play

one   hop

said   bed

number   fun

tree   rain

stop   lumber

train   we

Building Spelling Skills, Daily Practice • EMC 6682

Fill in the missing words.

> | trip | say | tree | train | number |
> |------|-----|------|-------|--------|
> | hop | said | stop | one | stopped |

1. Dad _____, "Let's go out for a pizza."

2. Maria rode a _____ to her grandmother's house.

3. I saw a bunny _____ to the carrots and then _____.

4. Martin was _____ _____ in the bike race.

5. They _____ by an apple _____ to rest in the shade.

6. What did the teacher _____ to her class?

My Spelling Dictation

Write the sentences.
Circle the spelling words.

1. _____

_____

2. _____

_____

Word Study

Double the last consonant and add **ed** to write
a new word. When a word ends in a vowel and
one consonant, double the last consonant and add **ed.**

1. trip _tripped_   7. pin _____

2. stop _____   8. plan _____

3. hop _____   9. slip _____

4. pat _____   10. chat _____

5. clap _____   11. skip _____

6. hum _____   12. drum _____

Complete the sentences using words you just made.

1. Ann _____ down the street.

2. He _____ on the ice.

3. Dad and I _____ a trip.

4. The man _____ his hands.

       Building Spelling Skills, Daily Practice • EMC 6682

Spelling List

This Week's Focus:
- Spell words with a final **k** or **ck**
- Review the two sounds of the vowel digraph **oo**

STEP 1 Read and Spell	STEP 2 Copy and Spell	STEP 3 Cover and Spell

fold

1. stick

2. trick

3. back

4. zoo

5. root

6. quick

7. look

8. looked

9. pack

10. cook

11. _____
      bonus word

12. _____
      bonus word

Visual Memory

Fill in the boxes.

stick	trick	quick	back	zoo
root	look	cook	pack	looked

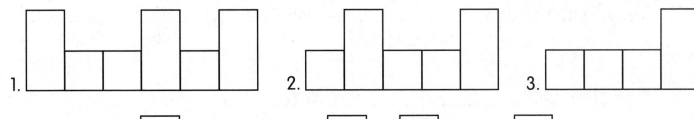

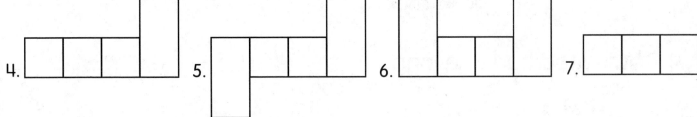

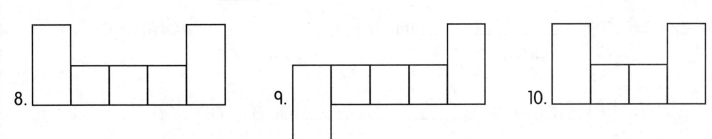

Rhyming Words

Match the words that rhyme.

stick	back	trick
look	quick	tack
pack	tool	cook
root	book	shoot
school	boot	pool

Word Meaning

Write the missing words on the lines.

1. Roy _____ for his homework.
   look, looked

2. Mr. Green did a _____ with a big _____.
   trick, quick   zoo, stick

3. The chef will _____ dinner.
   look, cook

4. That weed had one long _____.
   cook, root

5. Put the _____ in the _____ of the car.
   pack, look   cook, back

6. Will you help me _____ for my book?
   look, cook

My Spelling Dictation

Write the sentences.
Circle the spelling words.

1. _____

   _____

2. _____

   _____

Word Study

Listen for the vowel sounds.
Write **k** or **ck** on each line.
k becomes **ck** after one short vowel.

sti_____	clo_____	coo_____
du_____	boo_____	bri_____

loo_____   qui_____   ba_____

tri_____   pa_____   loo_____ed

Draw a line to match.

zoo

look   • /**oo**/ as in **hook**

root

cook   • /**oo**/ as in **spoon**

Spelling List

This Week's Focus:
- Spell words with the blends **pr**, **br**, and **ft**
- Spell two-syllable words
- Review long **a** words with silent **e**
- Spell words with the initial consonant digraph **ch**

STEP 1 Read and Spell

STEP 2 Copy and Spell

STEP 3 Cover and Spell

fold

1. birthday

2. people

3. present

4. candle

5. cake

6. children

7. gift

8. party

9. game

10. bring

11. _____
   bonus word

12. _____
   bonus word

Fill in the boxes.

> people   present   candle   cake   children
>
> birthday   party   game   bring   gift

1.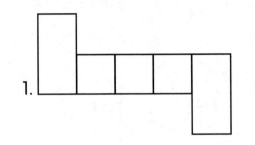

2.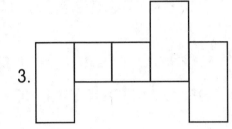

3.

4.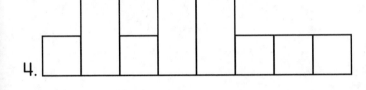

5.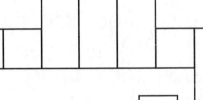

6.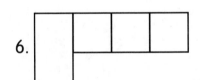

7.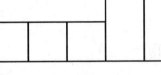

8.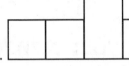

9.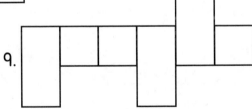

10.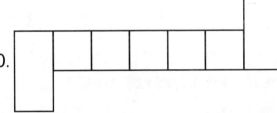

Fill in the missing syllables to make spelling words.

1. _____dle

2. _____dren

3. pres_____

4. _____ty

5. _____day

6. peo_____

Building Spelling Skills, Daily Practice • EMC 6682

Word Meaning

Answer the questions.

1. Are children people?　　　　　　Yes　　　No

2. Do **present** and **gift**
   mean the same thing?　　　　　Yes　　　No

3. Can you eat the candles
   on a birthday cake?　　　　　　Yes　　　No

4. Will your mother let you play
   a card game in the house?　　　Yes　　　No

5. Do people bring presents
   to a birthday party?　　　　　　Yes　　　No

6. Is your birthday the day
   your pet was born?　　　　　　Yes　　　No

My Spelling Dictation

Write the sentences.
Circle the spelling words.

1. _____

   _____

2. _____

   _____

Write **pr** or **br** on each line.

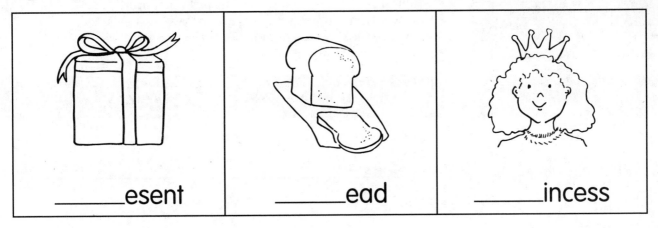

_____esent   _____ead   _____incess

_____etty   _____ize

_____ing   _____own

Look at the picture. Read the word aloud. Listen to the beginning sound.
Write the sound you hear at the beginning. Write **c** or **ch**.

_____ildren   ____an   _____ain

_____air   ____at   ___ake

Spelling List

This Week's Focus:
- Spell words with the vowel sound in **put** and **could**
- Spell words with the diphthongs **ou** and **ow**
- Recognize the short **u** sound in **something**

STEP 1 Read and Spell	STEP 2 Copy and Spell	STEP 3 Cover and Spell

fold

1. put

2. push

3. pull

4. could

5. would

6. found

7. round

8. around

9. something

10. brown

11. _____
    bonus word

12. _____
    bonus word

Fill in the boxes.

> put   round   pull   could   would
>
> found   push   brown   around   something

1.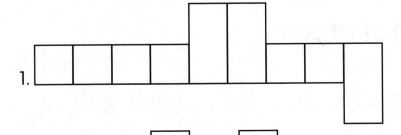

2.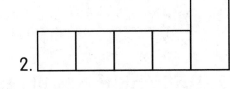

3.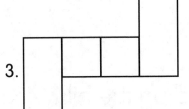

4.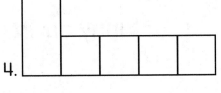

5.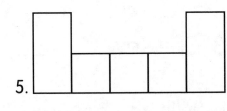

6.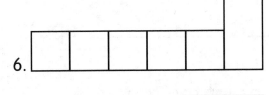

7.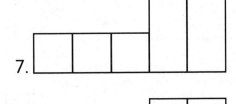

8.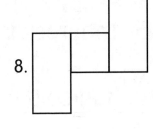

9.

10.

Spell Vowel Sounds

What is missing? Write **ou** or **ow**.

1. f_____nd

2. r_____nd

3. br_____n

4. cl_____n

5. ar_____nd

6. c_____

7. s_____nd

8. c_____nt

9. c_____ld

Fill in the missing words.

> put   round   pull   could   would
> found   push   brown   around   something

1. Otis _____ his lost dog.

2. Betty hit the ball and ran _____ the bases.

3. She saw _____ funny on TV.

4. Will you help me _____ my sled up the hill?

5. That rock is _____ with _____ spots.

6. Burt said he _____ help paint the fence.

My Spelling Dictation

Write the sentences.
Circle the spelling words.

1. _____

_____

2. _____

_____

Word Study

Read the words. Listen for the vowel sounds.
Write each word in the correct box.

round	put	push	brown
could	hood	sound	pull
town	now	would	found

the sound of **ow** in **cow**	the sound of **oo** in **wood**
_____ _____	_____ _____
_____ _____	_____ _____
_____ _____	_____ _____
_____ _____	_____ _____

Write a rhyming spelling word.

1. bush

_____

2. would

_____

3. full

_____

4. crown

_____

5. hound

_____

6. sound

_____

Building Spelling Skills

WEEK 29

Spelling List

This Week's Focus:
- Review long and short vowel sounds
- Listen for the initial consonant digraph **th**
- Spell two- and three-syllable words
- Recognize homophones (**no**, **know** and **to**, **two**)

STEP 1 Read and Spell

STEP 2 Copy and Spell

STEP 3 Cover and Spell

fold

1. they

2. their

3. many

4. any

5. anything

6. than

7. because

8. know

9. water

10. very

11. _____
    bonus word

12. _____
    bonus word

Fill in the boxes.

| they | their | many | because | than |
| know | water | very | any | anything |

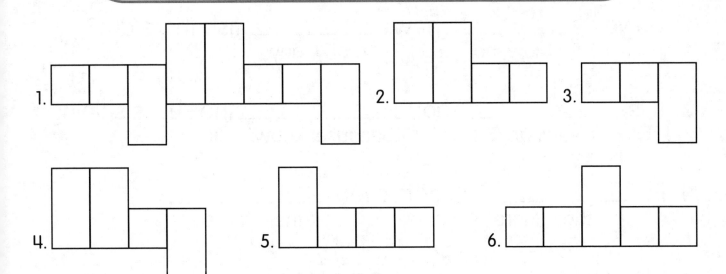

Find the Mistakes

Mark an **X** on the words that are misspelled.

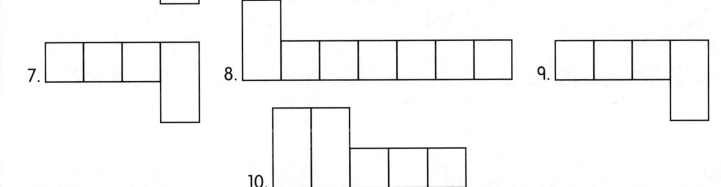

1. enything   anything

2. because   becuz

3. kno   know

4. thay   they

5. water   wadder

6. miny   many

7. verry   very

8. any   iny

Word Meaning

Write the missing words on the lines.

1. Grandpa said, "You may have _____ you want."

    anything, any

2. Do you _____ how _____ fish there are?

    know, no   many, any

3. It is _____ hot _____ the sun is shining.

    very, any   because, know

4. Put _____ coats over _____.

    their, there   their, there

5. When will _____ get here?

    they, them

6. Do you have _____ _____ to drink?

    any, anything   than, water

My Spelling Dictation

Write the sentences.
Circle the spelling words.

1. _____

    _____

2. _____

    _____

Word Study

Circle the sound made by the underlined letters.

1. th<u>ey</u>   a e i o

2. th<u>a</u>n   a e i o

3. an<u>y</u>   a e i o

4. kn<u>ow</u>   a e i o

5. n<u>i</u>ne   a e i o

6. ver<u>y</u>   a e i o

7. s<u>ee</u>   a e i o

8. c<u>oa</u>t   a e i o

9. pr<u>ey</u>   a e i o

10. s<u>o</u>   a e i o

11. man<u>y</u>   a e i o

12. m<u>y</u>   a e i o

13. pl<u>ay</u>   a e i o

14. p<u>ie</u>   a e i o

15. b<u>o</u>ne   a e i o

16. m<u>ea</u>t   a e i o

Homophones

Homophones are words that sound the same but are spelled differently.
Write the correct homophone on each line.

1. Do you _____ how to swim?
   no, know

   _____, you can't go swimming now.
   No, Know

2. I have _____ goldfish in my tank.
   to, two

   Can we go _____ the zoo next Saturday?
   to, two

Building Spelling Skills

WEEK 30

Spelling List

This Week's Focus:
- Spell words with initial consonant digraphs **wh** and **th**
- Recognize and spell antonyms
- Spell compound words
- Recognize the short **e** sound in **again**

STEP 1 Read and Spell

fold

1. which
2. where
3. there
4. before
5. after
6. over
7. again
8. inside
9. outside
10. under
11. _____ bonus word
12. _____ bonus word

STEP 2 Copy and Spell

STEP 3 Cover and Spell

Visual Memory

Fill in the boxes.

| which | over | where | before | after |
| there | under | again | inside | outside |

1.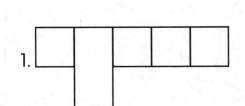

2.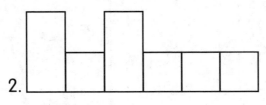

3.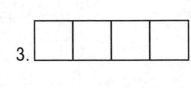

4.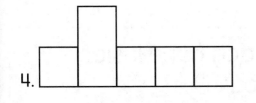

5.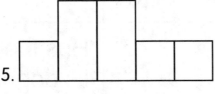

6.

7.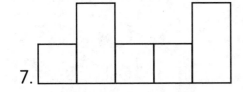

8.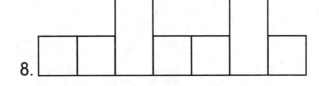

9.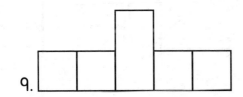

10.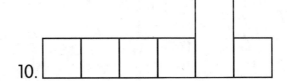

Opposites

Write the spelling word that means the opposite.

1. under _____

2. before _____

3. outside _____

4. here _____

Building Spelling Skills, Daily Practice • EMC 6682

Word Meaning

Look at each picture. Circle the answer to the question.

Is the cat hiding
under the bed?

Yes
No

Is the clown before
the elephant?

Yes
No

Is the cover over
the birdcage?

Yes
No

Has the dog gone inside
its doghouse?

Yes
No

Will you wear your raincoat
when you go outside?

Yes
No

Will you need a bath after
digging in the garden?

Yes
No

A compound word is two words put together to make a new word.
Make compound words here.

1. out + side _____

2. in + to _____

3. be + side _____

4. no + thing _____

5. birth + day _____

Write the missing words on the lines.

1. _____ place would you like to visit_____?
   Which, Where   before, again

2. _____ will you go _____ school?
   There, Where   after, over

3. We will go _____ _____ it rains.
   over, outside   before, inside

4. _____ are two frogs _____ the tree.
   There, Over   before, under

5. We walk _____ the bridge to go _____
   over, again   inside, there
   the fort.

Building Spelling Skills, Daily Practice • EMC 6682

124

My Spelling Tests

Using Your Spelling Test Forms:

First

Use the following pages for your Friday spelling tests. Write your answers on these forms.

Then

Record your score on your spelling record form on pages 156 and 157.

Spelling Test

Listen to the words.
Write each word on a line.

_____
date

1. _____

2. _____

3. _____

4. _____

5. _____

6. _____

7. _____

8. _____

9. _____

10. _____

11. _____

12. _____

Listen to the sentences.
Write them on the lines.

1. _____

_____

2. _____

_____

Spelling Test

Listen to the words.
Write each word on a line.

_____
date

1. _____

2. _____

3. _____

4. _____

5. _____

6. _____

7. _____

8. _____

9. _____

10. _____

11. _____

12. _____

Listen to the sentences.
Write them on the lines.

1. _____

_____

2. _____

_____

Spelling Test

Listen to the words.
Write each word on a line.

_____
date

1. _____

2. _____

3. _____

4. _____

5. _____

6. _____

7. _____

8. _____

9. _____

10. _____

11. _____

12. _____

Listen to the sentences.
Write them on the lines.

1. _____

_____

2. _____

_____

128

Spelling Test

Listen to the words.
Write each word on a line.

_____
date

1. _____

2. _____

3. _____

4. _____

5. _____

6. _____

7. _____

8. _____

9. _____

10. _____

11. _____

12. _____

Listen to the sentences.
Write them on the lines.

1. _____

_____

2. _____

_____

Spelling Test

Listen to the words.
Write each word on a line.

_____
date

1. _____

2. _____

3. _____

4. _____

5. _____

6. _____

7. _____

8. _____

9. _____

10. _____

11. _____

12. _____

Listen to the sentences.
Write them on the lines.

1. _____

_____

2. _____

_____

Spelling Test

Listen to the words.
Write each word on a line.

_____
date

1. _____

2. _____

3. _____

4. _____

5. _____

6. _____

7. _____

8. _____

9. _____

10. _____

11. _____

12. _____

Listen to the sentences.
Write them on the lines.

1. _____

_____

2. _____

_____

Spelling Test

Listen to the words.
Write each word on a line.

_____
date

1. _____

2. _____

3. _____

4. _____

5. _____

6. _____

7. _____

8. _____

9. _____

10. _____

11. _____

12. _____

Listen to the sentences.
Write them on the lines.

1. _____

_____

2. _____

_____

Spelling Test

Listen to the words.
Write each word on a line.

_____
date

1. _____

2. _____

3. _____

4. _____

5. _____

6. _____

7. _____

8. _____

9. _____

10. _____

11. _____

12. _____

Listen to the sentences.
Write them on the lines.

1. _____

_____

2. _____

_____

Spelling Test

Listen to the words.
Write each word on a line.

_____
date

1. _____

2. _____

3. _____

4. _____

5. _____

6. _____

7. _____

8. _____

9. _____

10. _____

11. _____

12. _____

Listen to the sentences.
Write them on the lines.

1. _____

_____

2. _____

_____

Spelling Test

Listen to the words.
Write each word on a line.

_____
date

1. _____

2. _____

3. _____

4. _____

5. _____

6. _____

7. _____

8. _____

9. _____

10. _____

11. _____

12. _____

Listen to the sentences.
Write them on the lines.

1. _____

_____

2. _____

_____

Spelling Test

Listen to the words.
Write each word on a line.

_____
date

1. _____

2. _____

3. _____

4. _____

5. _____

6. _____

7. _____

8. _____

9. _____

10. _____

11. _____

12. _____

Listen to the sentences.
Write them on the lines.

1. _____

_____

2. _____

_____

Spelling Test

Listen to the words.
Write each word on a line.

_____
date

1. _____

2. _____

3. _____

4. _____

5. _____

6. _____

7. _____

8. _____

9. _____

10. _____

11. _____

12. _____

Listen to the sentences.
Write them on the lines.

1. _____

_____

2. _____

_____

Spelling Test

Listen to the words.
Write each word on a line.

_____
date

1. _____

2. _____

3. _____

4. _____

5. _____

6. _____

7. _____

8. _____

9. _____

10. _____

11. _____

12. _____

Listen to the sentences.
Write them on the lines.

1. _____

_____

2. _____

_____

Spelling Test

Listen to the words.
Write each word on a line.

_____
date

1. _____

2. _____

3. _____

4. _____

5. _____

6. _____

7. _____

8. _____

9. _____

10. _____

11. _____

12. _____

Listen to the sentences.
Write them on the lines.

1. _____

_____

2. _____

_____

Spelling Test

Listen to the words.
Write each word on a line.

_____
date

1. _____

2. _____

3. _____

4. _____

5. _____

6. _____

7. _____

8. _____

9. _____

10. _____

11. _____

12. _____

Listen to the sentences.
Write them on the lines.

1. _____

_____

2. _____

_____

Spelling Test

Listen to the words.
Write each word on a line.

_____
date

1. _____

2. _____

3. _____

4. _____

5. _____

6. _____

7. _____

8. _____

9. _____

10. _____

11. _____

12. _____

Listen to the sentences.
Write them on the lines.

1. _____

_____

2. _____

_____

Spelling Test

Listen to the words.
Write each word on a line.

_____
date

1. _____

2. _____

3. _____

4. _____

5. _____

6. _____

7. _____

8. _____

9. _____

10. _____

11. _____

12. _____

Listen to the sentences.
Write them on the lines.

1. _____

_____

2. _____

_____

Spelling Test

Listen to the words.
Write each word on a line.

_____
date

1. _____

2. _____

3. _____

4. _____

5. _____

6. _____

7. _____

8. _____

9. _____

10. _____

11. _____

12. _____

Listen to the sentences.
Write them on the lines.

1. _____

_____

2. _____

_____

Spelling Test

Listen to the words.
Write each word on a line.

_____
date

1. _____

2. _____

3. _____

4. _____

5. _____

6. _____

7. _____

8. _____

9. _____

10. _____

11. _____

12. _____

Listen to the sentences.
Write them on the lines.

1. _____

_____

2. _____

_____

Spelling Test

Listen to the words.
Write each word on a line.

_____
date

1. _____

2. _____

3. _____

4. _____

5. _____

6. _____

7. _____

8. _____

9. _____

10. _____

11. _____

12. _____

Listen to the sentences.
Write them on the lines.

1. _____

_____

2. _____

_____

Spelling Test

Listen to the words.
Write each word on a line.

_____
date

1. _____

2. _____

3. _____

4. _____

5. _____

6. _____

7. _____

8. _____

9. _____

10. _____

11. _____

12. _____

Listen to the sentences.
Write them on the lines.

1. _____

_____

2. _____

_____

Spelling Test

Listen to the words.
Write each word on a line.

_____
date

1. _____

2. _____

3. _____

4. _____

5. _____

6. _____

7. _____

8. _____

9. _____

10. _____

11. _____

12. _____

Listen to the sentences.
Write them on the lines.

1. _____

_____

2. _____

_____

Spelling Test

Listen to the words.
Write each word on a line.

_____
date

1. _____

2. _____

3. _____

4. _____

5. _____

6. _____

7. _____

8. _____

9. _____

10. _____

11. _____

12. _____

Listen to the sentences.
Write them on the lines.

1. _____

_____

2. _____

_____

Spelling Test

Listen to the words.
Write each word on a line.

_____
date

1. _____

2. _____

3. _____

4. _____

5. _____

6. _____

7. _____

8. _____

9. _____

10. _____

11. _____

12. _____

Listen to the sentences.
Write them on the lines.

1. _____

_____

2. _____

_____

Spelling Test

Listen to the words.
Write each word on a line.

_____
date

1. _____

2. _____

3. _____

4. _____

5. _____

6. _____

7. _____

8. _____

9. _____

10. _____

11. _____

12. _____

Listen to the sentences.
Write them on the lines.

1. _____

_____

2. _____

_____

Spelling Test

Listen to the words.
Write each word on a line.

_____
date

1. _____

2. _____

3. _____

4. _____

5. _____

6. _____

7. _____

8. _____

9. _____

10. _____

11. _____

12. _____

Listen to the sentences.
Write them on the lines.

1. _____

_____

2. _____

_____

Spelling Test

Listen to the words.
Write each word on a line.

_____
date

1. _____

2. _____

3. _____

4. _____

5. _____

6. _____

7. _____

8. _____

9. _____

10. _____

11. _____

12. _____

Listen to the sentences.
Write them on the lines.

1. _____

_____

2. _____

_____

Spelling Test

Listen to the words.
Write each word on a line.

_____
date

1. _____

2. _____

3. _____

4. _____

5. _____

6. _____

7. _____

8. _____

9. _____

10. _____

11. _____

12. _____

Listen to the sentences.
Write them on the lines.

1. _____

_____

2. _____

_____

153

Spelling Test

Listen to the words.
Write each word on a line.

_____
date

1. _____

2. _____

3. _____

4. _____

5. _____

6. _____

7. _____

8. _____

9. _____

10. _____

11. _____

12. _____

Listen to the sentences.
Write them on the lines.

1. _____

_____

2. _____

_____

Spelling Test

Listen to the words.
Write each word on a line.

_____
date

1. _____

2. _____

3. _____

4. _____

5. _____

6. _____

7. _____

8. _____

9. _____

10. _____

11. _____

12. _____

Listen to the sentences.
Write them on the lines.

1. _____

_____

2. _____

_____

My Spelling Record

Week	Date	Number Correct	Words Missed
1			
2			
3			
4			
5			
6			
7			
8			
9			
10			
11			
12			
13			
14			
15			

My Spelling Record

Week	Date	Number Correct	Words Missed
16			
17			
18			
19			
20			
21			
22			
23			
24			
25			
26			
27			
28			
29			
30			

158

You are a SUPER SPELLER!

Super Speller

Name

Congratulations!!